A
Multicultural Song
that I Sing Alone

Bo Kyung Kim

AuthorHouse™ LLC
1663 Liberty Drive
Bloomington, IN 47403
www.authorhouse.com
Phone: 1-800-839-8640

Published by AuthorHouse 01/15/2014

ISBN: 978-1-4918-3222-6 (sc)
ISBN: 978-1-4918-3220-2 (hc)
ISBN: 978-1-4918-3221-9 (e)

Library of Congress Control Number: 2013920270

Any people depicted in stock imagery provided by Thinkstock are models,
and such images are being used for illustrative purposes only.
Certain stock imagery © Thinkstock.

This book is printed on acid-free paper.

Because of the dynamic nature of the Internet, any web addresses or links contained in
this book may have changed since publication and may no longer be valid. The views
expressed in this work are solely those of the author and do not necessarily reflect the
views of the publisher, and the publisher hereby disclaims any responsibility for them.

Contents

Part 1
Multicultural Songs

Part 2
Love Songs

Part 3
Nature's Songs

Part 4
Peace! Peace!

Part 5
Songs of the Motherland

Dedication

For all war victims including the civil war victims of the
U.S., indentured servants and forefathers in the early settling
immigration period of the U.S.

Acknowledgement

The word called love is always not tired. Wherever we are, whenever we listen, we find that we do not get tired of love. But the practicing of love is hard. For over 20 years, as I have lived in the U.S., I have experienced all kinds of life, death, hardship and pleasure, those stories stored in my deepened heart. Now, I release some of them out to the world. Some of them are rotten, and some glance back at me with a look eye of spite, while others remain quietly within my heart, as they had never been hurt. Am I, myself really, a more shameful, severe existence, at certain times having more thorns than a thistle flower? We all have elements of good and bad. Feeling too shameful, exposing myself and all parts of my bare body, I fear showing my face to the public. I devote this book to our American ancestors, first immigrants and many war victims, and I ask them to forgive me for my lack of love, and that I am sorry for living, sorry for writing.

I give thanks to staff at Cal State University Los Angeles' Writing Center for helping me translate these poems to English. Thanks to all the tutors including Shane and his staff that gave their spare time to fix grammatical errors. I also thank ISW members of Pasadena branch members including Jane Neff Rollins that gave me advice, all CSULA Political Science professors, Dr. James Lee and my two daughters, Sarah, and Jennifer, for assisting my English writing and helping me with others. I give appreciation to all of them.

Part 1

Multicultural Songs

A Multicultural song that I sing alone.

Climbing to the top of the mountain of Griffith Park,
Singing a song that a long, long time ago might have been sung and disappeared.

The life and stories that
From the opening world,
There might exist a little microorganism floating in the water
With bright sunshine that
Has to move to another place.
And roaring lions and zebra herd's voices in the savanna.
And different flowers' love stories.

Songs from long time ago, the ancient history of the human world,
From ancient Greek city states and Roman civilization and
European bravery, Asia, Africa and the Americas,
Many ancient states' peoples' vivid lives.

Like Korea's ancient state, Gaya's immigrants went to Silla ancient country
Like a small stream flowing into a river.
Songs for those exertions, sweating and bleeding from Africa,
Europe to America for landing and
Passing across the Atlantic Ocean.

Like a sunflower turning its head to the sun.
After a seed is buried in the ground
The environment of the sprout is no good,
The little sprout has to cry a lot,
And wishes to move to an another place.

I am singing a song of the long, long wandering, and bleeding
Shining beauty and sad spring songs,
The endless songs that are never enough to sing and sing
And singing but disappearing,
Lost nomadic songs.

Multiculturalism
Thou permanence, and
Endless flowing river,
And long journey songs.

To Socrates

If I were born in Ancient Greece,
I might have been an ardent student.
However, I am happy living in the present
Since two thousand years have passed.

I would rather have pure justice, just good justice.
A Pure thing, a right thing,
A thing that cannot divide or be split.
One is beautiful, two is ugly
Many is beautiful, however, dangerous because it can be weak.
Whenever we see the dropping of one big water drop,
After it falls down, breaks, and scatters all around,
It becomes weak, and finally disappears.

I know that disappearing doesn't really mean disappearing.
And it is good to remain a shadow.
However humans like the present world
One love becoming two loves is upsetting,
And two loves becoming one love is beautiful.
And I want to live in a one love justice where love never disappears,
And shines permanently.
I want to live in that big, one justice.

The U.S is all about accumulating and spreading
Money, power, and thoughts like that in your ancient Greece.
There is no device that unifies those dispersed things.
We need one great justice that covers these parts,
As a flying bird picks its food hidden somewhere,
We have to find the great one that is hidden in our place.

Multicultural song 1.

Bloomed. A flower bloomed.
Multiculturalism bloomed in America.

A peach flower, an apple flower, an orange flower
Every branch of the tree
Colorful, colorful
White, yellow, black and red
And with many mixed colors
Here, there
This place, that place,
This corner, that corner
A big flower, a medium flower and a small flower

A Christmas tree where all little flowers bloomed
And decorated, hung with many special ornaments.

Bloomed. A flower bloomed.
In an American continent,
The flower of multiculturalism bloomed.
In this place, in that place,
A flower has bloomed as many shiny shapes,
Flows into the world river meandering
Shii shii shii shii
Flow into Europe, Asia and Africa leisurely.

The whole world sees it.

Multicultural song 2.

Oh my goodness.
I have never seen bugs swarming:
Gun killings, drugs, rape, alcoholics and gambling.

All of this,
Because of You.

We can draw splendid paintings
With only red, yellow and blue colors.
We can make an excellent menu
With only bread, meat and vegetable soup.

You are fascinating,
But tedious.

As you encroach on my soul
And infest me with diseases.
My nose is losing its sense of smell
My eyes hardly see
Going blind.

You are so tired,
Multiculturalism.

Multicultural song 3.

You are so tired.

Even though a lotus flower blooms in dirty mud,
It is very hard to remove dirt fully everywhere.

Many honey bees, many birds fly into here
Many poisonous spiders, cockroaches
Invade everywhere
Before flowers bloomed, their sprouts rot and die
The dirty perfume spreads everywhere
Also, the parts of your body have to be pruned cruelly sometimes
It is a war in beauty.

Multiculturalism
Even though, it is not your noble name
A beauty exists inside a unit
Part and whole is the one,
Just as there is the front and back of paper.
Like many dirty things, death and severe pain
We have to fall down and
Wander often
Between life and death
Under your lofty name of coiled thread.

Multiculturalism
How about taking a rest and yawning
Behind a little plant.

Multicultural song 4.

Wah! What flower is this.
I never saw a flower that had
Many small, different colored leaves in my life.

Beautiful.
The genes that shine bright like a rainbow
Your colorful light is the peak of the best goodness and optimal beauty

Constantly taking off your skin and dividing cells, creating great life
But, there is one rotting piece of humanity in the shadow.

I wish everything were designed properly,
Even the dark shadow optics would hang down,
The shining light that the dazzling star lit—rainbow
And shining dews of sunshine.

Multicultural song 5.

A blooming flower has to have a bee. That is life.
Damn it. There is no beautiful perfume in this flower is
What is the reason.
That is insufficient nutrition or the incorrect temperature.
Sunlight and water are necessary.
Some flowers, in the blooming process, die.
Some, in their blooming process, might break.
Nobody knows.

Which level of a Californian multiculturalism?
We need to check if the perfumes blow well or not.
If water and nature's fertilizer are proper or not in
Our garden's flower.
All drying up in the Garden of Eden, we need to check again
We need to consider that cut up flower branch
The pressure to hurry up,
To over fertilize in order to bear fruit quickly
Different people, colors that decorate
A flower leaf, a piece of flower
Thou favorite loves.

Multicultural song 6.

Trying to dance Korean Bongsan mask dance.
Raise a hand, hit, twist, throw in any direction
Purity, natural things, originality is broken,
And all mixed, destroyed and
Then creating the melting pot and so,
Making it something different and new.

You are destroying and creating missionaries
And a love magician who is satisfying that destroyed, stepped—on
Natural, clean originality.

What color is thy climax.

Multicultural song 7.

I don't want to melt.
I want to remain myself in my essence.
But like the blowing autumn leaves by an autumn wind
Like the pebbles of tough ocean water
Like the new figure created that was cut and trimmed by a thousand years,
Everything has a fortune that has to change.
However, I want to live just myself, in my natural shape.
Like the pubescent girl who has long hair
Even though I have suffered, attacked by all kinds of wind and rain
Like the dauntless pine tree
That never changes its green color for a whole year,
I want to remain a pure being.

Multicultural song 8.

Ripened.

Multiculturalism was in Kimchi.
And in a Burrito.

Like a ripening persimmon
Like a ripening apple
Also a ripe grape ripens wine rightly

With many vegetables, decorated with various carrots, garlic,
Radish and many kinds of fish sauce and cereal,
And make it have a good taste.
Burrito which is like my native Jeju's food;
Bing—Dduk which means round rice cake that
Has many vegetables, bean sprouts and long pieces of radish
And cover them with a round tortilla.

How about the taste of American multiculturalism?
That is, decorated with many minority cultures on the bases of Europe
And gun culture; the smell of perfume is properly ripe
And bloomed beauty, something short and insufficient.
That is
Gun culture, a little inappropriate,
Gives people some happiness but some ugliness.
Is it a contradiction of democratic multiculturalism?
Democracy pursues, protects people's lives,
But many civilians become victims due to guns.

From inside a red rose, emerges a black bug.
A little unnatural, a little broken.

Multiculturalism !, So, nevertheless, you get an A-

Multicultural song 9.

It's because of you.
In this world that is full of beautiful miscellany,
The guy named cockroach, one day he came into this place,
Laid eggs which bred, multiplied, and made more war.

All of this is because of you
A giggling baby gets angry and gets tougher
Demanding juice, candy, and chocolate more than milk.

It's because of you.
The things that I have loved, the things I have achieved,
With such burning passion, and put them down,
Tonight, I fight back with a book and
Live a youthful life, even though I have aged.

All of this
Is because of you.
Multiculturalism.
Ah, I'm tired. Tired.

Multicultural song 10.

-Flower-

I want to go back to my grandfather's land.
Because I couldn't be a good bloomed flower and you
Don't allow me to play the part
In this beautiful cast
In this beautiful paradise.

No matter, not a single flower
Has to bloom two or more divided flowers
In the process of growing, it has to soak nutrition from other flowers,
How tragic and sad it is!
No, my entire nature itself, my enriched beauty,
Diversity and all my property being taken by yours,
Crying, crying and
Begging in front of other flowers.

I want to go to my native home village
In there, by myself
With only my energies
I can make a single beautiful garden.

Multicultural bird.

-To Dr. Siler.-

You said I should focus on one thing,
But I fly here, there, everywhere.

You are right. I am a multicultural bird.
I don't like saying this to anyone, nor showing it.
Really, I don't like people. Rather, I love people.
However, I can't meet people.
Because, situations don't allow me to.

I also am a part of nature, dews, trees and flowers.
All I can do is whisper.
And I can't do anything
As a human, and not human,
Like a multicultural goddess and a spirit
Who I have to create many different colored fruits and
Who droops and falls down by bearing too much heavy fruit.

Making many different fruits in one tree.
The fortune of an American tree.
The tortures, the fantasy and happiness
What can I tell you.

Just every, every day, I ignite fires that burn.
And make energy, give them to the people for free,
How can I tell you.

Today, still I can't stay in one place.
Wandered here, there, and gave birth, too many seeds
Of time that exist here and there,
And don't exist anywhere with a permanent language.

As I am saying, one thing is a whole and
I am living in a huge life composed of small little things.
The life of a multiculturalism's tree.

White cloud

I am staying near thee.

Like the phrase of poetry any poet
Who "as the moon goes with the cloud,"
Like the crossing of the sun and moon in an eclipse
I will stay and leave, hang in the sky of your parking lot.

It is April 8th, on Wednesday, around 2PM.

Wearing a costume of shiny material
And wearing a white peace cloth.

Thou might be busy, and
Can't see passing white clouds
Due to other reasons.

Like all human life,
Because people are not free, by the iron chains
Of money, honor and all life work.

Maybe, thou, while I stay
Come to me saying "Hi" or "how are you" or not
"Nice to meet you again"
Can give me a light greeting.
And might be telling me good bye.

Or not
Thou just might murmur that
"Oh, that is the white cloud I saw before,"
Which might pass, ignored.

I am passing near you.
Fretful and sad
I stayed near you and passed.

Even though there might be a few eclipses
Of sun and moon, in a life
Seeing the parting and anticipating seeing it again

Multicultural colored sacks are filled
A little bit heavy, also holding a peace flag,
The cloud will pass.

American flower wagon

There are the cultures of Europe, Asia and Africa that
Dance together with the melting temperature of the body
With cold language and igniting fire
In the place where winds cross
Between the northwest wind of the Atlantic Ocean
And the northeast wind of the North Pacific Ocean

Whites are among whites together
Koreans are among Koreans together moduru*k**
Greeks are among Greeks together moduruk
Circled, sitting down, and lit up
The passionate mind that makes a flower garden.

Between different cultures
It might be discordant, however,
Even if it makes a harmony,
It is a flowing river.

The reeds in a field rely on each other
The wagon is heavy with pushing, pulling,
Goes to hold many colorful flower sacks on its back
Can't run
Ee-reh-chak, Jeoh-reh-chak*
Getting stuck here, getting stuck there
The left side is staggered, also the right side is staggered,
This side creaks, that side creaks.

Falls down and gets up
Crash! It finally falls down.
Really, at this time we might have to call a doctor.

In the place where winds cross
Between the North Pacific Ocean and the Atlantic Ocean,
The colorful flower wagon is groaning.
Like the fighting in the wide field alone
Against the strong north wind,
America is groaning alone with many problems
Such as the war on terror, human welfare and gun problems.
Holding a cross of world peace on its back
Ee-reh-chak, Jeoh-reh-chak
.

* "Moduruk" means similar things grouped together. It refers to when sprouts emerge from seeds all together at once from a melon thrown in the backyard. Dialect of Jeju, South Korea.

* "Ee-reh-chak, Jeoh-reh-chak" means to be stuck, trying to move forward but being unable to. And trying different directions, zigzagging, but being unable to move forward, because the burden is too heavy. Dialect of Jeju, South Korea.

Great love

Regardless, I need to take care of my baby
I should take care of the other baby first.

A person, who wears Korean dress, does Korean dances
Studies the Brazilian Samba dance and Peruvian Vaca Ratay music.

Loving something is
Not loving myself and my possessions,
Loving other people and giving them everything unconditionally.

Even when I am sick and don't pursue myself
Pursue other's thing and become united

Even though I can't eat,
I feed others first.

At the moment of dying
I think of other people.

Then, they learn about ours and
Becomes ours.

Loving is not just giving to others extra energies or work,
But to give all exertion and devotion.
Even if it takes your soul and everything
Just give everything.

Creation exists inside of destruction.
White purity in new things blooming
As an eternal flower.

The great love is.

On the freeway going to Palmdale and seeing desert 1.

Oh my goodness! I forgot to lock my house door.
I want to go back home.
I don't want to see your power.

How can I.
The night suddenly comes without notice.
The autumn comes without notice.

Are you okay
Such a proud
Absolute figure.

Right.
I have deviated.
What are you going to do to me.

On the freeway going to Palmdale and seeing desert 2.

Even I am getting old
You thoroughly destroyed all my hope.

Yesterday, I heard about one woman
Who is the wife of a medical doctor,
Fifty two years old, and is pregnant.
I also have a hope, the amount of a slight thread.
You burnt all my young energy.

I don't want to give up
Even though I am old
I want to hold a flag against your perfection.

This is not it.
I am alive.
My youth is rising and waiting.

Your love was perfect.

Meaninglessness

-Playing Piano Concerto No 1. Of Rachmaninoff-

There is a poet who wanted to play piano well.
Every day, she played piano like a person trapped in hypnosis
Put her hands on the piano keyboard
Practiced piano until her eyelashes become white.

The music was
The Serge Rachmaninoff's Piano concerto No. 1.

She heard a voice saying that
There was no meaning to playing piano.
Or that she was only wasting her energy.

Look at that. She heard it.
Telling her, "hum, you are stupid."
You are doing a second creative art.
You already have a first creative art.

She complained to Rachmaninoff
Because she has small fingers.

Finally concert day came.
Another pianist performed for her accompaniment
Instead of an orchestra.

Two pianists played piano
The give and take of a melody.

But how should we do it.
In the middle of the performance,
She forgot the music notes she had memorized to play.
The audience was silent.

She opened a music sheet, and quickly played but
Was unable to completely finish the first movement.

In the end, staying up all night to practice
Had become meaningless.

She has to be born again in multiculturalism.
But she doesn't want to melt.

Part 2

Love Songs

The elegy of autumn

Standing alone by the window on a rainy day
I heard the footsteps of someone who left to go far away
With the last leaves remaining from the burning site
And with my head bowed
I'm quilting every fragment of my unfinished verses.

No matter how I outlived
Even whenever my legs were struggling
Like the spout of water that flows underneath and underneath
Like the misty rain that vanishes into a whitish spray
Our lives seemed to be the same.

The man who loved, loved is gone forever
And won't come back.

Ah. As the fallen leaves weeping
With reddish tears on autumn days
All things that I love disappear from me go far apart.

A autumn leaf letter

Sending you a letter made from a red leaf that
I send to the wind.
Holding contents
I couldn't write.

Yesterday
Severe wind blew.
I sat down on the top of the tree
And I saw death come and go
Over the tree.

To a floating cloud,
I murmured something and
To the flowing water
Spoke cynically that

Living is
Not only misery.

I loved only you.

Now, daytime goes and
Nighttime comes
I won't be sad anymore.

The field that thou left
Wind blows and snow falls
Holding the mountain shadow
Hugging evening dusk
Silently approaching thy thinking
I will play with them.

Tonight is short.
Wishing you could be happy.

Equation of love

Thou are a star
I am a moon.

We are flowers of the universe
Bloomed again
Washed with the water of the earth.

Permanence is very far.

We are flying birds
Lost our way
Looking for the contradiction of endless freedom

As I exist
You shine
As you exist
It gets dark

Undefined equation
That has lost a half.

Short meeting long farewell

The reason I can't meet thee is
The fear of the ceasing to yearn for thou.
Like a star far away from us
Our love looks far away
I will always stay near thou.

As a shiny star,
Even rainy wind strikes your window
As a floating cloud,
As a turning wave,
Wandering, meandering,
I will stay in thy heart.

Which star did we come from,
Meeting together as flowers of a little moment and
Needing to disappear as morning dew.

A star and a star
Even though, it is at a distance of millions of light years.
Thou!
My soul who is longing for thee
As a whisper of wind,
As an evening dusk,
Staying in a leaf of a tree,
Will knock on thy window.

The meeting that was just a couple of minutes
I forgot to say to you that I love you forever
I have to ride the farewell train that sad, far away
Without promise, and final destination.

Even though I can't meet thee

Even though I can't meet thee,
It doesn't mean I leave thee.

Fearful punishment after a short meeting with thee
I will accept it happily.

Like the shaking tree,
As the pain of yearning patiently endured
Even I call thy name painfully, pitifully
But it comes to me only as echoes.

In the standing state,
Becomes a flower.
One poet said if someone endures yearning patiently,
One become a star.

In the standing state,
Becomes a rock.

After waiting, waiting
Blooms
A white gourd flower in the night.

Thou.
In which field, are you wandering now
Having become wind.

What loving is

The reason why I couldn't leave thee is that thou and I are one.

Like water encounters water and flows together,
A cloud meets a cloud, and flows
The root of reed and branch grow from one

Inside my heart, thou become bone and flesh,
And grow into branches and
Breed and make a nest.

The reason why I couldn't put thou far away,
Thou are my native home and place to rest.

What loving is, is not only someone yearning someone.
It is a dancing pose that has lost its native home,
That looks for their roots, and
Wants to stay together.

Farewell

Without saying good bye
We have to be apart.

The day that red leaves fall down
Like a flower—rainfall
The day which the strong autumn sunshine pours
In the space between lovers
And tears sprinkle, have to be apart.

Please don't forget me.
Can't bear to see thy tearing eyes
Becomes a bird that lost a wing,
As a sadness like
As if the earth is sinking
Each has to be scattered into a different side of the sky.

Be happy
Be healthy
Bye.
After thou left, said those words,
Sobbing, like the spreading halo of the moon.

Without saying good bye, we have to say, set apart.

With a pain like the world is sinking,
The day when red leaves flew like peony flowers,
We have to part.

To baby 1.

-For the first daughter Sarah-

Baby, I want to go inside your smile.

You turn on a light and carry morning sunshine through
Blue dreams from dark streets and gloomy forests.

Shivering of green sprouts.
Dew drops of plants.
The bird that woke up from morning sleep
And chirping sounds.

Baby, I want to go inside your clear blue eyes.
The sound of the sky opening.
Pouring rainbow colored sunshine.

Passing through the field of crunching reeds,
Crossing a white cloud,
The pieces of pains of the stopped wandering in past days,
As a burning, passionate flower.
Holding the dew of the early morning.
And a bloomed flower warmly.
You are the angel of light wearing a white gown.

Baby, I want to know what you are muttering.

Perfect love

If thou treated me well, as a true love
The Mediterranean Sea would flow
And wet Europe.

The Atlantic Ocean flowed
And wet America.
The Pacific Ocean flowed
And wet Asia.

If you treated me well, as a true love
Not only stars in the sky and the moon,
But also all people in the whole world might have been happy.

There might have been no bloody war.

Camellia

-In front of the library of the Cal State University Los Angele-

You don't need to burn like that.

Nobody will look at and smile at you
Even if you cried for a thousand years.

Time burnt thee
And mixed it with dust
It still remains burning ashes
And again a flower blooms
Nobody gives you a smile.

What is your essence.
Are you a wind that
Wanders between lovers,
Or a shining early morning star
Or an evening dusk that hangs in the sky and
Makes colorful the whole world.

Burned by drought
From early dawn until the sun sets
Has to be burnt,
Your fortune is unavoidable!

Cried for a thousand years
Bloomed for a thousand years
Again wandering and waiting for a thousand years,
Your red tears.
The cold smile and sadness.

Red rose 1.

1.

Want to cry
Want to call
Finally you are sobbing a black, bloody color.

More lonesome than a true seeker's pain,
Than a wanderer,
Saying to the passing white cloud
Even if, if I fall down, I won't despair.

You, who loves permanence.

Your tears that are pouring out are just
Tears from deep hurt.

2.

Even though, the set-aside darkness,
Like the emperor of thousands of years
You are the fountain, unaffected by drought,
Your desert doesn't dry up.

Finally, you won.
Your enduring patience never ends.

For the one time birth,
Burned reddish rising,
Holy is your soul
It decorates a house's garden.
Which season does you rule.

In this painful time
Heals alone
As a silent hurt deeper
Than the winter sea
Sublimating,
Revival
Flying, you are the
Eternal phoenix.

Red rose 2.

In the season of the rose,
I think about the meaning of the rose
Blooming in every garden.
Surrounding, there were bloody leaves flying everywhere,
And a groaning sound comes to my ears.

When Korean General Lee Soonsin, died in a battle with Japan in a war
in fifteen ninety two,
And when he was shot by the enemy, he told his soldiers to cover his
body with a shield.
And not to show his death to his other soldiers.
He was worried that his soldiers' morale would sink.

Then how about American soldiers in Iraq.
They fight against evils under The War on Terror.
It is the same as General Lee's case.
While we live comfortable lives,
Somewhere, someone has become a victim of evil for our happiness.
The rose leaf of the victim comes to my heart and begs.

I planted a rose flower deep in my mind.
And gently it makes me reflect.
I planted it every day and it makes my life new and revived.
And evaluate whether my life has been greedy, selfish, or full of hatred.
Many red flower leaves fall onto the ground.
And whenever the rose flower leaves fall,
I check to make sure that I didn't do any wrong today.

Blood falls from the sky today.
I didn't do anything today.
Damn it. I might not even pray for the people and war victims.

Part 3

Nature's Songs

The song of earth

-Groaning sound of nature-

My body already raped
I want to die, my limbs are being torn apart.

Keeping a pure soul
Suffering from all kinds of pollutions
There persists one spot of hope like a thread.

As getting fall down
Try to get up
As getting become dirty
Try clean up more

Again, the stair of hopelessness,
One, two goes down
Making more move down,
However,
Cannot get up.
Cannot produce a life.

Cutting flesh in my deep heart
Ruining my metabolism and

Cannot making sing a warm, spring song
Cannot give birth to a life, one speck,

Rather, I want to die.
And leave my bleeding body here.

The houses on the top
of the mountains

-The groaning sound of mountains,
passing by the 405. S Freeway to San Diego-

Ah—ha ! Those guys!
You sit down on my head.

How dare you.
You sit down on the top of the sky and
You cut the top of my head.

For your survival
I supplied you energy, clean air,
The dew of the morning washes your soul,
And green leaves cool your summer heat.
For thousands of years.

Now, you sit down on my head.

How rude you are
Are you going to be a god like that.

You might be happy with that
I am dying, bleeding

For your happiness
I am victimized
Cutting my body
You don't recognize this.

Palm tree 1.

-Gazing up at the Palm Trees-

Isn't it high time
You humbled yourself.

You've been enduring long wailing hardships,
Standing tall in the air as a towering giant.
It's the very time to descend.
Though you had them bloom for a moment
Up there against high winds,
Wouldn't they break soon enough.

Going through tests, trials and tribulations
How hard you've been pressed and pressured.
You still bounce back like a spring
Looking like you're about to snap and break.

Armed with life experiences and wounds,
Wearing all around a heavy outfit looking like scales
You look all the more skinny.
While walking on thin ice before
Never did you fail to focus on the inside.
Breeding a winter of sublimation
You soared to the sky, to the sky.
At long last,
You have bloomed, Miss Towering Beanpole.

Now you will have to stay.
Setting aside the dream of flying
Burying love and passion
Lighting a lamp quietly
Singing a song softly,
Isn't it high time
You danced the most beautiful dance.

Palm tree 2.

Did you hear the sound of the gun.
Still you are magnificent.

As you are shivering with fear
As you boast to us of your nobility
You look like an unchanging four season greenly pine tree or
The four nobles of the oriental.
Apricot, bamboo, orchid and chrysanthemum,
You really are the young aristocrat.

Like the coming and going of the seasons
Like the surfing of blue water in the Pacific Ocean
Posses the noble dignity
You are the king of plants in the world.

I feel shame
As I think of leaving here
To another place from such little fear.

Palm tree 3.

How long have you been enslaved.
How long have you been stuck in a pained environment.
And tortured by cold and parched by hot weather.

Don't cry. We also are the slaves that left our native village
And they had hard lives.
Like the American ancestors who came to James Town, died of dysentery
As they had drunk impure alkaline water
Like the Ancient Korean state, Gaya, its immigrants' enslaved lives,
By conquering a neighboring ancient state;
The Silla dynasty that become to unify the Korean peninsula.

Look at the American land.
Wasn't everything transported like you.

We also are floating clouds and foreigners
That pursues happiness over the mountains and
The people who came to this land
And followed the bluebird.

Is there anything that is not transported from somewhere.
From Europe, Africa, Asia and all of the world,
Coming from everywhere
Swept onto American land.

So don't cry please.

Song of dandelion.

How happy
I am.

Tanning in the spring sunshine all day.
Kissing with the wind
Making a pillow using the grass-texture that whispering,
Lying down, my body is tired
Srrrr . . . * begin to sleep,
Full heart
Singing of the cobalt sky
I am a wanderer of the earth.

Even though,
I may have just a moment of fortune

The rustling of the spring wind
My perfume flies lightly everywhere
Even if the autumn wind dries up my body and it disappears
Inside the black darkness,
Dream again of beautiful festivals and
A wedding
To ride a splendid flower wagon,
Preparing for tomorrow's best spring event
What a happy woman I am.

*"Srrrr": the sound of falling asleep. Korean.

The song of adjective

I like adjectives.
In the morning, I get up, and
Secretly avoiding my master's eye,
Line up with them and slightly run away from them.

From far away wind rises
A flower blooms

Wandering between crowded people
Swimming in the sea
Laying eggs in the forest
In proper time, stopping work is okay.

Ah. How freely happy I am
But we cannot talk only that way.
The past day they suffered in the corner
If someone should have need of me,
Must run to them.

Can't receive love from anyone,
As an abandoned slave,
How much I cried bitterly for many days,
As a soundless flower.
For how many old and long winters
Did I desire to become the backbone and
Main stone of buildings
To become shining first place.

How many times did I fall down
From climbing cliffs and stony mountains.

After too much strong exertion,
Again falling off and doing it again,
Lost my way, fighting and fighting,
My whole body shone from all the scars
Colorful, colorful.
He, who became the most beautiful pearl in the world,.

But, his fortune is not only bad.
Because of the adverb that comes to us slowly from far away.
Even though, it's not too strong but
There are existences worse than him.

As the power to move conquerors
Seen, not seen, but a bird that stands and sings a song
On the stage, makes the whole event more wonderful
It's an invisible, helping hand,
The extras in the cast that complete the production.
Like mothers working behind-the-scenes,
I like adjectives the best.

In one spring morning

Because the late coldness is very vigorous
I yelled "you guy!"
Then, suddenly scared a magnolia flower
That cried and shed a tear
And just bung-gut* smiled.

* "bung-gut": to open mouth and smile. The state of a flower blooming. Korean mimetic word.

Spring morning

Spring mood comes and goes everywhere
Gga-bul gga-bul* frivolously playing around

Birds singing songs.
Jjong! Jjong ! Jjong!*
Use stacatissimo* and counting beats,

Stream water flows,
Jol jol jol*
The vibrating sound of the cello doing scales

My baby mommy mama mom mom
Singing a song in a foreign language.

Dead tree sprouts again
My soul's trees keep a silent language for frozen winter
A little bit shivering, wings go bu-shi-shi*, wake up from sleep.

Seeing a spot of light from far away
How spring wandered the cold icy fields,
And wandered deep in the valley of despair.
In order to share with the world its spring light.

The morning of the first spring
I dusted off the dust that had gathered in my soul during the winter.
Today, I fixed a broken watch for a long journey.

* "Gga-bul gga-bul": refers to a state of frivolity and playfulness. Korean.
* "Jjong! Jjong ! Jjong!": refers to the sound of birds chirping. Korean.
* "stacatissimo": a word from music meaning to have short, clip sounds.
* "Jol jol jol": refers to the sound of a stream flowing. Korean.
* "bu-shi-shi": refers to wakening up from sleep. It is used when people wake up
in bed, rub their eyes or touches their hair or face to clear their minds. Birds and
animals do this too. Korean.

Winter chrysanthemum

The baby chrysanthemum that
Lays on the icy ground.

Like walking on a sharp knife
After passing the railroad

It seemed that spring's warm sunlight
Was shining on the hill.

Procrastinating from being missed
Blooms a flower, a sprout

Where are gone the times
That spread fresh flower perfumes,
The soul keeps this flower garden alone.

You are the protector of the winter that
Weaves the season,
With tears of despair from waiting and waiting.

Conversation with a flower of tree.

-At the CSULA campus, seeing a flower tree-

You speak to me.
I have a hard life.

But even so, you are patient.
No matter how difficult your life
There was a hope like a thin thread
For the future.

If I always live my life modestly,
I could obtain a little seed of a flame of desire
I can have a seed of happiness.
It tells me to wait more,
And to never forget to smile.

-Studying at the university again-

Broken wagon

When are you going to finish
Pushing Sisyphus' stone.

When I climbed the mountain,
It falls down.
I climb again,
Again it falls down.

The broken cart can't go
But needs to go ahead
With one wheel

Ri
    di
       cul
          ous.

Oh, my goodness
There is a common sense.
Is it okay to push such a broken wagon recklessly.

Part 4

Peace! Peace!

Peace Dance dedicated to
The Civil War Victims of the U.S

Dead
Alive

Fall
Get up

A flower
Blooming
From the blood spilled,
In the back of flowing past history.

It is the scream of an unknown girl,
Trampled
By horses of the Civil War.

No, that might be the dream of
A disappeared southern soldier,
The gesture of a soaring Native American Indian
Who was killed by bullets
In an early settlement.

Or not, that might be
The love story of an indentured servant
From Europe.

Or that might be
The mournful song of
A slave from Africa.

You are alive,
You never died.

Your bloody sacrifice
Now blooms into white flowers, and
Flows into the waves of a white river.

Sometimes it moves powerfully,
Quietly, and silently.

Risen up,
Twirling,
Healing the painful times
Of a thousand of years of America land.

Dead, alive
Fall down, again get back up.

Dance for the indentures servants past gone

-For the people who have undergone indentured servitude in the Americas.-

For thee,
I am devoting this rose.

From Europe or Africa, far away,
Looking for a dream, happiness and freedom
Came to this new land.

As you loved
Wandered
And collapsed together
You all disappeared together.

For thee, in here
I light a candle.
The sound of hope that crosses over death.

Blown by a wind,
Moments of oblivion that
Cross over the deep blue waves
And the Atlantic Ocean.

Finally flew to this new world,
As a light in America's heart.
Became a white bird
Landed on this America land and
Became the blooming white flower.

For thee,
I am devoting this dance.

Fallen, dead and alive
Permanently
Living forever with descendants of America
Eternal, the most beautiful,
Living forever dead but unable to die
Thy dance and life.

I am devoting this dance,
Here.
Now.

Dance for Cleopatra 1

Cleopatra whom I met yesterday
Said to me,
My love is early spring weather.

For thousands of years
She's wandered
And wandered
Transcending time and place.
Standing in the alley into which early summer strode,
She said to me,
I've betrayed love many times.

Love and ambition
Her hidden stories that still remain unmentionable
She buried those deep in the Mediterranean Sea.
She gave up on her dream to capture the Mediterranean region
in the face of love for two men.
Destroying my pride that I had great love,
She said to me,

My love wasn't honest.

White migratory bird

-Planning for peace dance performance tour-

I want to stay,
But I have to leave.

At the new place,
Making a nest
Laying eggs like
Lilies, snow and moonlight
As drinking white dew
Have to lay my eggs here, there and everywhere.

After hatching many eggs
They fly to the sky quickly all together
The world becomes a white color, and ugly things
Like death and violence will disappear
And the world will be clean.

I want to stay
But I have to leave.

At the new place,
I have to lay eggs, and make peace
Without death by guns and war.
And I have to lay many white eggs
That cover the conflicted world.

A song of the Korean Peninsula 2.

-Thinking of the world system-

Can we ride
The brilliant golden wagon.

Sitting on seats of the
Old, shabby and smelly
Train of democracy.

Pushing, pulling
Exertions that go ahead
To visible first class seats.

Bleeding scenes that
Tried to see the bright light
In the lighthouse.

Sometimes having the chance to get lucky
Close to the seats in first class
Sometimes like receiving a glorious award, then
Quickly falling into the fireplace.

The will that goes ahead again
Healing burnt hearts.

However
If we play a game together
It has to be a fair game
It shouldn't be a gamble.

As seen in sports
It has to have a fair referee.
Is there any game without a referee.
Of course, even if it has a fair referee,
They make mistakes.

So, our show onstage, the name of the world system
Would always remain to be uncompleted homework.

Then, although it is not shining,
The golden wagon
Even though it is not the last, worst seat
With shouting and fighting

Always given as an award are
The middle seats
The second class in
The train of democracy

Hearing Aristotle's
Middle way is better

Even if we, in the second class seats,
Shall we clean the dirty, old democracy train
Into a new and clean train?

And shall we do space travel
With all people
More safely and beautifully.

To mother

Mother,
Please let me stay
In one place safely.

Tears from wound
Scratched by stumps,
My whole body
Covered
In bloody scars.

Far away
Far roads
Too tired,
Why do you make
Me travel again?

Mother,
Please let me sleep
In one place quietly.

I don't want
To betray you anymore.

Even if it
Rains,
Snows,
Spring goes,
Summer comes
Spring comes again and
Snow falls, covering the whole world again,

I want to stay
In one place.

I am happy
With once love.

-Playing the Piano music of a 'Frantz Lizt Etude de Concert No. 3
farewell to music and toward studying Political Science-

Generally people live one-way lives. If we live a one-way life how beautiful it is. Living is traveling. I loved poems, and being a musician, and a dancer. However, when I say farewell to all these things I have loved, how can I express the misery?

Life is a continuity of farewells. My life is the same as well. I want to be a good pianist. I played the Piano Concerto No 1 of Tchaikovsky and same number of the Rachmaninov. I devoted all my passion. I wanted to live in a musical world. However the boat of my life changed the direction. I play Liszt farewell music and it means starting another world. And among the music I played, Liszt was the last music that I played on the piano. Now I am studying world history and political science, and majoring in my future. Since then, I haven't been able to play piano anymore and I have to say good bye to music. I wrote this poem on the piano keyboard directly, while I was playing Liszt piano music Etude de Concert No. 3, the last song I've played on the piano.

Magnolia that bloomed in January

Hey. Look at you.
Smiling loosely.

Really you are hasty.
Still, everyone is sleeping,
Some of them are still drunk,
Red leaves hang on their bodies,
And prepare to sleep for winter.

Yet, it is freezing January
Are you going to give birth to
The messenger of spring,
Announcing hope.

An overdue baby is no good, but
A premature baby causes worry too.

You must be really greedy and imprudent.

No matter how fast you run,
You will be in the same place,
And regardless of how fast you finish your work,
It will be full of mistakes.
Don't you know that that's logic.

Don't be so proud of yourself.

Spring ladies who are giving birth babies
Before marriage ceremony!

For Robert Frost

The empty house on North Canyon that I visited,
Thy son lived and decorated the front and back yard
With many kinds of citrus trees, avocado trees.
Thou stayed in this house
Where on the fence coiled twisty grape vines,
Hung bunches of grapes,
And fruits from nameless trees.

If I lived here the rest of my life
I could play with thee.
Walking in nearby mountains, forests
And waterfalls freely,
And we could share stories about life,
Stories about peace and love.

Now, thou art gone,
And although you felt nostalgic for
The road you couldn't take,
I wandered among many roads.

Thou focuses thy energy only on writing poetry,
But I come and go
Among music, poetry and dance.
Especially, around the philosophy of multiculturalism.

And I stayed a bit in the music world, playing piano,
Performing dances
For achieving peace and
Writing poetry and
Even more, studying in a university,
So I could share with thee
In the human dream
That couldn't be achieved by thy soul.

Since thou left fifty years ago,
In the forest thou walked, still
The season, like a fog, stayed and went,
The sound of the mountain waterfall
Is the same as before,
A California morning.

That dry cough,
Vomiting,
Due to the high price of gas
And the stagnant economy.

How wonderful it is,
This meeting between an Asian female poet and
Robert Frost who refused his fame,
And hid here, writing poems.

In this small house filled with grape vines,
I am contemplating thee silently
For a while, with thy poems.

Spring festival

-For the blooming flower tree,
In front of Beverly Hills High School, as I dropped off my daughter-

Shi!
Stop. Please.
As spring comes,
You are so fussy.

Just wait a little longer.
You could have a more severe painful moment.
Soon, you might experience painful, burning sensations,
And it might be the worst moment of your life.
You will be in a state where you can't feel alive or dead.

Even though, right now, you think your life is happy.
Don't behave too carelessly. Gga-bul-ji-mah*.
You might never hear the H of Hope.

So, you girls and boys.
Don't be fussy.
Please stay quiet.

* "Gga-bul-ji-mah": a command meaning to play around or to not take things
seriously. Korean.

To baby 2.

-For the second daughter, Jennifer-

From the beginning of the world,
You were a flying bird
That was eating a dream.

One day when the red leaves were
Blowing like snow flakes
As it was falling into more blue hopelessness,
You approached me.

The day I fell down
Sick from autumn and
Carried into the hospital on an ambulance
Like in a fantastic opening of the universe,
You sat down in my body.

Just sleep well.
All I can do for you
Is to just pray with my two hands together.

Even if the sky sinks,
Staying at your side only.

Gun Sanjo

*Sanjo is one of Korean traditional solo music that has free form like an epic poem in poetry.

In the U.S,' life demands
That we be stronger.
Be stepped on by others.
We cannot protect ourselves
This can be evil.
We have to protect ourselves and from others
Especially if we cannot do it by ourselves
It can be sin
Being beaten is a sin

The world makes Narcissus get a gun.
Peace only exists between peaces
Not violence.
At least, the gun inside our heart
Narcissus, however, doesn't want to carry a gun,
If not, Narcissus will be a victim
Really, should she carry a gun.
If she possesses a gun,
Around her someone, anyone, a family member or others
Can be victims.
Narcissus doesn't want anyone to become a victim due to her gun possession.
Narcissus also didn't know about her bullet possession.

Becoming an American citizen is like
Being married with America.
Like the butterfly that flies under the name of love,
Jumped into a flaring fire,
Narcissus couldn't get a house, a husband
All of her happiness lost,
All of her rights of her husband and child
Were taken by a gun,
Taking care of herself alone
With two girls, without money, with empty hands
And depression.

Is this a civilian's life in a democracy.
The world
If we have to have a gun, is
About survival and being treated well by others.
People naturally can live without a gun,
The world is contradicted by natural law
Really, is this world a just society.
Is the U.S. a democratic country.

Is there any peaceful country where Narcissus can live without a gun.
Nowhere except her grandfather country Korea.

Just as a clean, beautiful mind stays silent,
It can easily be a victim.
And then it can sin,
Cannot protect Narcissus herself and cannot be responsible,
And has to be treated badly.
Really, does Narcissus have to carry a gun for survival?

In Korea, there is an old saying
Knives call knives.
If others pick up a knife
That someone dropped in the street,
And keep the knife,
They will die by a knife.
If someone carries a gun,
The person who carried a gun has a high chance of dying from a gun.
However, the higher risk of dying lies with the weak, poor, pure, gun-less person.
What can the reasons for this be?

Walking in the street thinking silently,
Seeing signs that say "Armed response"
Standing in a flower garden
In many residential neighborhoods.

In a moment, Narcissus say
"Wow, it is scary". And immediately Narcissus felt her soul burning.
Are people really happy with such a threat
To the passing people or a neighborhood.

Narcissus wanted to hurry to some quiet place and
Go to a safe country with no guns or war,
That guaranteed our survival.
Naturally, the safe country is one where one doesn't need to possess a gun,
And doesn't feel the need to forcibly carry a gun.

Now, Narcissus fights between two ways,
Gun possession and none, going back and forth many times.
Where will it be.

Like a Native American tribe,
Shall Narcissus go into the forest and live.
We cannot avoid the State's system and society.
But Narcissus wants to go in the forest,
And should Narcissus live a life like the native tribal people.
She is looking for a safe country.

Narcissus has a right to live well with her daughters.
All her rights, property and freedom taken away by a gun.
Couldn't demand her rights,
Because, if she demanded her rights, she feared revenge from them
Lives as slaves,
Forgetting all human rights, property, freedom and happiness.
But it wasn't in Korea, her motherland.
In Korea, there is no civilian gun possession.
Narcissus' life was honorable, good and she had a lot of pride.
Narcissus knows compared to the Sandy Hook victims, her life is nothing.
She has to appreciate everything about her life;
Even if is like the slave's life in paradise.
Is it really paradise?

Really, if we can live by possessing guns, the gun is not a weapon and
Can be a tool of protection like the messiah for our survival
Then, poets, musicians, and dancers should carry guns,
When Narcissus is performing art,
And everyone should carry a gun.

However, Narcissus believes that the blooming flower always falls in the end.
War will end someday.
Because, there are no eternal ones in this world.
All things are only a moment blowing in the wind,
Even, nature or existing things try to mature
From unnatural imperfection
Into perfect completion.

As if, if the weather is hot, we have to take off thick clothes,
We change to wear thin shirts.
After the passing of a tough rainstorm,
Continues clean weather.
Narcissus will wait for spring of next year
Wearing greenly, thin, hopeful cloth.

Evening dusk shows her that,
Hot weather will still continue tomorrow,
And it looks like the blood of forefathers of America.

Studying environmental international law

What we define as justice is not justice.
It is only the incomplete things' dancing pose.

Water flows from upper to lower
We cannot resist the flowing water.

Like a flower talking to a flower,
Like a star talking to a star,

We have to ignore the mystery of language and
Follow flowing water or time.

What we call truth is not truth anymore
It is only the loved and
Burned mark of ashes.

Truth, justice and democracy, all of these things,
Any of these is a blooming incomplete pearl,
Created in a silent wave,
For thousands of years,
From the light of death, reaching completion
That in shyness, of little light,
Which has the color of the sky.

The reason of studying political science

There is no completion
If we don't pass through the dark tunnel.

Love and hatred, also no achievement,
If we do not pass the ordeal and
Through the valley of hardship.

Why I am studying political science is
There are many reasons,
At least, for learning the theory, I recognized,
That the theory is positive, negative and goes to positive.

Look at the festival of flowers.
Even the whispering of nature and
The rolling of the ocean waves.

They might pass the passage of hard trial.
And they might pass the passage of a difficult history's curve.

The reason the poet, dancer and musician has to
Study political science is to achieve life,
From the most beautiful life, pass the worse ugly life
And to return its beauty to the final goal of life,
For achieving the finishing of
The sonata of life and
The symphony of life.

For the gun supporters.

Knowing five taste senses through the tongue
You are rose trees to bloom.

The contradiction of passion,
Freedom, beauty
And life will.

Part 5

Songs of the Motherland

A Song of the Korean Peninsula 1.

With my waist cut, I have lived for over sixty years.
Now I don't know, the upper half of my body
What is going on.

As I lift my head, see the sky,
There is unlimited space
Standing as a lower body that has been divided.

Don't have an upper body
So, definitely don't have head and heart
What shall I do.
In that situation, just make a head and a heart
And dance calmly in that state.

With only half of a body, I can do everything.

As I live like that
It is fun to fantasize of being a living creature.
It almost seems dead, but not dying easily.

With my waist cut, I have lived
Over sixty years.
I don't know
What's going on in my upper body.

After the cut,
New sprouts have grown up densely and
To find an upper body and connect,
Cover the whole upper body.

Wishing that the cut weren't
A permanent fate.

Divided Korea 1.

There was no wrong,
Fighting between themselves,
I don't want to see it anymore.

No matter, in order to bear a fruit,
A plant makes a flower
With lots of sweating and bleeding

The news says to my ears that there is
Only bleeding without fighting against

I don't want to hear it anymore.

Water flows from high to low,
Runs to the river and sea
The cold North West wind—chilled
Goes down and
Takes the hand of the South Wind

There was no reason,
Being divided into two bodies
Hurting and fighting each other
I don't want to think about it anymore.

Divided Korea 2.

Oh, how dirty!
The leftovers of the Cold War.

Stick to the body deeply.
Never coming off.
Can't move.

Can we cut the Pacific Ocean with a knife.
Or can we cut the huge strong wind
Blowing onto one side
Into two.

Anyway, you are severed
Divided, rotten,
The leftover rotten smell sticks to my nose
Causes disease.
Even though people are dying,

You never move.

Now, do you know that
Your purity becomes a sin like this.

Writing a poem in Korean 1.

Reading an English book,
For the best improvement of English skill
Never use the Korean language.
From conversation to writing, all full of English.

Just the Korean identity.
If I lose my Korean identity,
Isn't it okay, because I am living in America.
As I live in America, I should use English.
English is not another language.
It is my language.

Reading a book.
In between English letters,
Korean letters come and go.

In the night sky, like the many shining stars,
That stick in the sky,
Korean and English letters look like the Milky Way.
Black, dark sky
White, one dot, come here and disappears
Blinking, it gets smaller and
Disappears quickly in the dark.

All directions are black world.
I also fall down.
My body, full of bumps,
Couldn't bloom flowers.

Writing a poem in Korean 2.

I already turned off a light
Where does the light come from.

One white butterfly
Comes to me silently,
Sits down inside my heart.

Still, the road is far away
The cold is strong
The butterfly comes to me
What does she want to do.

In the blackish dark,
You were alive.
In the various diseases and noises
That were scattered

Come to a place like this and
Sit down silently
What do you want to do?

Lovely my childhood friend.!
My friend.!
On thy heart, I put my hand
In thy heart, I remain as a white cloud
Withoutl promise.

We are going together.
You become a shadow of my heart
You take the same permanent road as well.

Dancing bird 1.

-For knowing who I am-

For knowing who I am
I wandered here and there many times
I was a dancing bird

Never fall down
Fly into the sky, into the sky, higher
I was a phoenix.

Writing some poems
And music
Dancing
Studying again in the university

Sometimes staying in tree leaves
Blame the world
And playing with them
Thinking with pity.

Stay with them
Go in the mountain
Go in the deep ocean
Existing, not existing
Staying with the dew of the morning
And disappearing quickly
Flower leaves or ocean waves
Come in and goes away,
An invisible bird

Living is the continuous dancing and moving
Without relation to death and destruction.

Today, I am still dancing.
I go to the ancient city state and
Climb up to modern society.
And from the deep ocean to the highest sky,
Dancing, singing songs, writing poems and
Studying and thinking alone.

Dancing bird 2.

-For flying highest-

To see farthest away
Have to fly the highest in the sky.

I have accepted, and endured patiently
Severe windstorms and air pressure
Evaporating misty air in clouds.

The world, I see from the highest sky
It is a small feather.
Round shapes, water drops.

It looks perilous, destroyed by footsteps,
And like the mighty blowing wind
Spreading many small sand castles

Inside there,

Ahong dahong* ahong dahong
Ahong dahong ahong dahong.

It is really funny.

*"Ahong dahong": a Korean mimetic word that describes human life, works or
events in human relationships like marrying and divorcing, having fun, fighting
and killing each other, laughing and crying over things in life. It means that
human things look very insignificant. Korean.

Riding a train.

For the first time in America, I rode a train to go to Long Beach.
The train was almost empty.
The seats toward the driver's seat were silent,
I sat down on a seat from where I could
See the front views through the window and
On the right side seat near the window,
Waiting for the train to leave.

A few passengers were waiting and looking at the view from the front.
Just a little later, the driver came and the train started moving with
The operating sound "broong"
Oh! oh! some people were confused, and laughed
Oh my goodness ! the train went backward.
People expected the train go to forward,
Obviously, the train should go forward they thought but it went
backward.
The first seat I sat in became the backward seat, and I ended up losing.

In life, the front is back, the back is the front.
Then what do we do.
In the world, there is no order.
If mine is yours, and if yours is mine,
It will be fair.

And our lives are one-ways that can't go back.
Going toward to death and going back to youth again
And like the train that goes back,
If our lives are the same getting old and getting young,
How will it be good.

All rules and laws in the world will be meaningless.
A permanent and never-ending life might remain.

Dancing Korean ancient court dance.

Going back to the beginning of history.
Rising up right hand toward the left side and
Rising up left hand toward the right side.
Like the positive and negative and
The plus and minus
Again two hands move to the center and
Rise up two hands making one,
From parts to whole
From division to harmony and unity.

In primitive society among Korean people.
Was there this harmony.
In and out, dead and alive
Two makes one, scattered
All things, like truth,
The stream connects to the river
And goes to the sea.

I draw ancient designs on the walls of buildings, caves, and temples.
It looks like the breath of Arabians
Or it looks like the breath of humanity.

Inside the dance
I become a stream and flow into the oceans.

And then this cycle would repeat eternally
Rest, stop, and revive.

Singing the Korean art song "Spring Lady"

At the Cal State Los Angeles campus,
In the snack shop under the flower tree which bloomed
With a cup of coffee
I am reading Michael Robert's "The Disposable Male"
And I am singing that Korean art song "Spring Lady"
Looking at that music sheet that was held between class notebooks,
I write English pronunciation in the music sheet, will sing the song later,
Suddenly I felt I was in heaven. A Song is,

"Spring lady comes by herself
She wears new green clothes.
She wears a white cloud veil
She wears pearl dew shoes,
Holding a bunch of flowers in her chest
Who is she looking for.
She comes to us."

The beautiful song like this,
The beautiful poetry phrase,
Why couldn't they keep to themselves.
Crying, crying, had to fight with others
Against Japan's rule in The Korean War.
The Korean ancestor who lived,
Enduring many tortures, pains through history

Summer! You ignore spring.
You built the summer house over spring, or
Planting a summer tree over spring.
You can destroy the spring's hope
Even if you decorate your house well, or
The summer tree produces many fruits,
You might be happy.

However,
The spring is the spring
The spring always has hope's breath
You will never change spring's lively hope.

Because, the beauty has beauty itself
Has to bleed in many cases
The truth had truth itself and has to be beaten,
The goodness has maximum value,
But has to bleed also
It will never change.

In the ocean, can we catch a bird.
And in the tree, can we catch a fish.

So,
The spring is the spring.

It will never change the spring's life
Even, the strong winter storm blows over there,

Spring has come.

Still, today, somewhere.
The beauty that couldn't bloom,
Might be crying.
While nobody knows.

Ganggang suwollae 1.

Flowing shaved line.
Thin nature and river.
Nation's breathing flows.

A Silk dress, red pigtail ribbon,
Jeo-goh-ri,* upper dress,
Worn beautifully,
The long skirt, Chi-ma* with twelve panels,
Stand with the head dropped, quietly,
Like the pulse of the history that continues, flowing
Hand in hand, taking hands.

Whenever each foot steps, every step go ahead,
As it splits up, releases, and again connects,
The thread coil of moderato's* Joongmori*.

Surging waves is the sobbing of thirsty reeds'
Standing on fields.

Huge wagon wheel
Let's quilt one, beads that turn
As dust that disappear into the permanent world.
The time turns back, inside knuckles of time
Several thousands,
Several hundred thousands,
Several hundred millions of years.

Echoing of a gong,
Flying the copper—colored inside of fog,
Beautifully spread dance's pose,
Sadness blooms and fades.
Inside cold winter, the crane is more pitiful.

The sad souls passed over the field of five thousand years
Connected like a legend, wandered in a circle,
Toward the opened place,
The upper strip on fingertips,
Ascend upwards into a deepened dream.

Becomes one with the universe.
Becomes one with an immortal god.

Is this a field insect crying.
And the flowing of a water plant.

Like the exploding sigh
The anxiety of screaming,
Riding the melody of a thread

Take off,
Becomes a crane,
Flies the world.

Turning this earth.

Being created, disappearing,
And again being revived.
Ganggang suwollae

Gang

      gang

           su-wol

                lae.

* "Jeo-goh-ri": upper dress of the Korean traditional dress for women. Korean.
* "Chi-ma": refers to dress. skirt.Korean.
* "Moderato": a word used in music to denote a medium speed.
* "Joongmori": means "middle speed." musical tempo in a Korean music.
* "Ganggangsuwollae" is a Korean group of women who, in a circle, sing and dance folk songs transferred from ancient tribe states. Wearing traditional clothing and holding hands together, they sing a song and make a circle pursuing the unification of community and harmony. The Korean Lee dynasty's general, Lee Sun-Sin used this dance in battle with Japan in 1592, winning the war with this dance. Ganggangsuwollae's meaning is "let's watch out for enemy coming to us." Korean.

Ganggang suwollae 5.

-To Thee-

Thou.
As thou are getting far away from me,
I will dance Ganggangsuwollae,

From eye to eye
From forehead to forehead
From heart to heart
Running, falling
I will love thee until torn.

As thou leaves far away
The sound of the tear bomb gets closer.

The snow—flowers of bloody—tear that has mixed
Falling down yearning,
In this continent far away
I will plant it beautifully step-by-step.

The day thou leaves,
Soul of a nation,
Over this long history,
The song that I couldn't sing in my native country,
I will sing.

Ganggangsuwollae 8.

Yearning becomes a reel,
Makes flower bloom.

A nameless girl becomes a butterfly,
And dances.

The soldier's soul that died and went,
The shaved line of nature that suffers from pain,
In people, far away,
White, Arabian and Mexican faces,
Form dews of sweat beading, song song song* in their faces.

Beautiful.
The dance of my native country.
The hopelessness, dead but cannot die, sticks
In any white woman's chest.

A yearning becomes a song,
Sing, and even fall,
It cannot falls down,
And sings in this far away place.

*"song" is a Korean mimetic expression of bearing drops of sweat on the face or in
other places of the body. So, song song song is the state of sweating.

Multicultural revolt

Visiting M city, which is not diverse, for teaching dance,
The day, blowing late winter-wind runs away,
To this side and that side, comes back
And hits the back of my head.

I was bitten by a flea
After one night's sleep in a cheap motel
That reminds me
Of feeling carsick
Of the slow, public bus of my native village.

The back of my hand, wrist, face and neck.
The traces of pains of memories scratched that I never saw before,
In here, there, and everywhere, as if resisting.

Nor, like looking to dig up a gold mine from mountain,
How the flea sucked blood from my body.

Maybe the flea is marking its territory or
Because I come from somewhere else.
Or Korean word; Gun-gei-il-hak, which means,
A crane of many chickens.
Means different one in similar things together.

What kind of thief you are!
You despise and assault me.

Tiny red little flea.
I hit the flea on bed, red blood comes out.

You!
You also a gun criminal that coming out
A black bug in a beautiful rose.

If you want to resist, do it.
I will never shake,
Even though, you bite me everywhere.

And it is okay my extra blood gives you some,
But what about the blooming garden.

Multicultural river will flow
Even if it is polluted,
Multicultural flower still blooms
Even if it suffers from all storms.

Tell me,
Is there any beautiful ideology.

How much did we bleed in the U.S. Civil War.
How much did we bleed in the First and Second World Wars.
How many American lives were lost in those two world wars.

That is the best goodness.

The M city looks quiet,
The early spring wind again hits the back of my head
And changed direction and
Blows in front of my body.

Cold air that
Feels like cutting flesh.

Devastated my skin.
Nature appears, hurt from gold mining,
Wraps itself over my ruined skin and
Disappears from my eyes.

Wind blows tough through the garden once again.
Some flower trees fall down.
I look at my devastated skin
And I pick up a light of hope that falls down.
And set it upright.
        * Other title name is "a flea's rebellion"

Lyricism and Chord of ontological idealism

A multicultural song that I sing alone

Tae Ho Kim

1. Introduction

The poet Bo Kyung Kim has most recently published the second poetry book Ganggang Suwollae: *a* Korean *circle [round] dance* (or the song for it).

She has been absorbed in writing poems ambitiously and positively in a busy life with a refined mind and a pure image and a sincere language (poetic word). In fact because she shows enthusiasm in writing poems so much with an evident sense of duty, she will realize that writing poems is her vocation as well as she is very diligent and has the convinced soul of poetry.

Without spilling so much of her energy completely, nothing can be formed in the various cultures and life as now—That's the way of the world.

From that point of view, even though anybody throws herself heart and soul in such phenomena, we should not overlook the fact that it is impossible to realize the meaning.

Without being born in the poetic talent, though she tries to reach her utmost, she can't write works which can impress any readers. In the true

98

sense of the word, there is only able to say that the works which do not convey impressions are not real works.

The poet Bo Kyung Kim now tries to publish the fifth ambitious poetry, A multicultural song that I sing alone and release the hopeful poetry drastically to the readers of the world with all kinds of enthusiasms and dreams. Her figure of trying her best is not only so affecting and encouraging but also secure and endlessly beautiful. Just in that sense we realize that literature is never a virtual image. At any rate, as Matthew Arnold says, 'literature is to express life artistically using languages.

If the works are not artistic, it goes without saying that such works don't have any meanings and values literarily. Einstein told that "what human beings have achieved and created till now is in the river of poem and love". It is really surprising and glad that a physicist not a literary man says like this. I think that a physicist recognizes the importance of literature.

We think that human beings need to confirm something in the poem.

What I want to emphasize here is that discovering and confirming the self through the object is our human being. Literature is to make the human life the expression in language precisely based on the principle of relativity. Therefore, it is true, of course, that the literary touches also can be accomplished on the basis of the relativity.

2. Poetry World of A Multicultural Song That I Sing Alone

Assuming that there is no perfect poem in the world, seven poems among poems in this poetry would be analyzed considering space limit. There is a standard that I refer to in order to analyze the poetic world of poems in the fifth poetry. Based on criticism of Matthew Arnold, a British poet and cultural critic, I mentioned "To see things as they really are" and "A poem is comments on life." to attack 'snobbism' and 'regionality' of UK while emphasizing traditional standards of European literature and clarifying social function of criticism. Literary criticism has become criticism on civilization, society and region, which is based on the criticism of Walter

Pater, a British essayist, literary and art critic. In particular, realism literature that values reality shows it in common.

A poem includes polysemy, which explains why each reader interprets it from different perspective. Likewise, different from the perspective of Bo Kyung Kim, the writer and a poet, a critic may interpret it from different perspective. It is because of the poem's characteristic that a poem is metaphor. Now we will examine the poetry world of "A Multicultural Song That I Sing Alone," the fifth poetry of Bo Kyung Kim, a poet.

Multicultural song 1.

Bloomed. A flower bloomed.
Multiculturalism bloomed in America.

A peach flower, an apple flower, an orange flower
Every branch of the tree
Colorful, colorful
White, yellow, black and red
And with many mixed colors
Here, there
This place, that place,
This corner, that corner
A big flower, a medium flower and a small flower

A Christmas tree where all little flowers bloomed
And decorated, hung with many special ornaments.

Bloomed. A flower bloomed.
In an American continent,
The flower of multiculturalism bloomed.
In this place, in that place,
A flower has bloomed as many shiny shapes,
Flows into the world river meandering
Shii shii shii shii
Flow into Europe, Asia and Africa leisurely.

The whole world sees it.

"Bloomed. A flower bloomed./ Multiculturalism bloomed/ in America." It sings that multiculturalism bloomed in America. The repetition at the beginning, "Bloomed. A flower bloomed." is to emphasize that a flower bloomed. It is emphasis in rhetoric. Repeating the same or similar phrase emphasizes the meaning of a sentence to inspire a reader or to reach the climax. It is called graduation. "A peach flower, an apple flower, an orange flower/ Every branch of the tree/ colorful, colorful/ White, yellow black and red" may mean that each race differs as what multicultural means. As a metaphor, a flower means multicultural. "—In an American continent,/ The flower of multiculturalism" Originally U.S. is a country that consists of immigrants from all over the world. Thus, U.S. is a diverse country. From the perspective, it may mean that a flower of multiculturalism blooms—i.e., U.S. culture diversifies with various cultures. Thus, it is an ontological witty poem.

Multicultural song 6.

> Trying to dance Korean Bongsan mask dance.
> Raise a hand, hit, twist, throw in any direction
> Purity, natural things, originality is broken,
> And all mixed, destroyed and
> Then creating the melting pot and so,
> Making it something different and new.
>
> You are destroying and creating missionaries
> And a love magician who is satisfying that destroyed, stepped-on
> Natural, clean originality.
>
> What color is thy climax.

-Full text of Multiculturalism.6

The mask dance mentioned the poem above means the traditional mask dance in Bongsan, Hwanghae, Korea. "Purity, natural things,/ originality is broken,/ And all mixed,/ destroyed and/ Then creating/ the melting pot and so," The Bongsan mask dance is a melting pot that breaks and recreates the purest and the most natural things. That is, the dance means a crucible—a place/country/state that synthesizes various factors including race and culture; in particular, U.S. Here you may find the real value of pure Korean mask dance before the territorial division. The poem understands the essence of a poem, which is why it is a very witty poem. Matthew Arnold said that "Literature is an artistic expression of life by language." I agree with it. Thus, I think it is an essence that art should not be art for art, but art for life.

A Song of the Korean Peninsula 1.

With my waist cut, I have lived for over sixty years.
Now I don't know, the upper half of my body
What is going on.

As I lift my head, see the sky,
There is unlimited space
Standing as a lower body that has been divided.

Don't have an upper body
So, definitely don't have head and heart
What shall I do.
In that situation, just make a head and a heart
And dance calmly in that state.

With only half of a body, I can do everything.

As I live like that
It is fun to fantasize of being a living creature.
It almost seems dead, but not dying easily.

With my waist cut, I have lived
Over sixty years.
I don't know
What's going on in my upper body.

After the cut,
New sprouts have grown up densely and

To find an upper body and connect,
Cover the whole upper body.

Wishing that the cut weren't
A permanent fate.

The poem regrets Korean Peninsula crippled deeply. "With my waist cut,/ I have lived for over sixty years." It explains Tiger-typed Korean Peninsula. "Now I don't know, the upper half of my body/ What is going on." It explains that Korea has maintained two countries under two different ideologies since it was divided into two through 38th parallel by developed countries after independence on 8/15. North Korea ruled by Ilsung Kim invaded into South Korea with tanks. Thus, war against each other was inevitable. It leads to significant loss of lives and destruction of many building and property. After truce, North Korea has still tried to invade South Korea and sent many spies. It also has committed terrors including sinking a ship, Steller's Sea Eagle, blowing up Cheonan ship and Yeonpyeongdo bombing. "Standing as a lower body that has been divided." It explains South Korea as a lower half from the 38th parallel. "After the cut,/ New sprouts have grown up densely and/ To find an upper body and connect,/ Cover the whole upper body." Considering that South Korea is much more developed than North Korea, it is expected that South Korea unites the nations. It suggests concern with the nations maintaining the division, not united. I think that the uniting nations are our significant mission. Ideally, the uniting two nations are inevitable for our descendants. From the perspective, this is a very refined poem phenomenologically.

Perfect love

If thou treat me well, as a true love
The Mediterranean Sea would flow
And wet Europe.

The Atlantic Ocean flowed
And wet America.

The Pacific Ocean flowed
And wet Asia.

If you treat me well, as a true love
Not only stars in the sky and the moon,
But also all people in the whole world will be happy.

There will be no bloody war.

-Full text of Perfect Love

It suggests that there is no one who truly loves their partner to risk their lives. That is, there is no perfect love with no shame. Because of human nature, variability, it is obvious that people change their heart. In a sense, some people selfishly pretend that they are in love to get what they want. It is true that it is hard to find someone who risks his/her life for love. It may make sense that people love politically. The poem is about perfect love, love for life. However, it is only a wish that is hard to find in real. It may be because a human is not God and does not have foresight. You may consider how hard-hearted the world is. "If you treat me well, as a true love/ Not only stars in the sky and the moon,/ But also// all people in the whole world/ will be happy." 'If you loved me truly' means the perfect love. The conclusion is that people would be happy with true love. Unfortunately, it is not what it is because of the human nature, being selfish. It may be considered endless sin of human beings that are greedy metaphysically and empirically. Thus, it is worthwhile deeply appreciating the poem.

Divided Korea 1.

There was no wrong,
Fighting between themselves,
I don't want to see it anymore.

No matter, in order to bear a fruit,
A plant makes a flower
With lots of sweating and bleeding

104

The news says to my ears that there is
Only bleeding without fighting against

I don't want to hear it anymore.

Water flows from high to low,
Runs to the river and sea
The cold North West wind chilled
Goes down and
Takes the hand of the South Wind

There was no reason,
Being divided into two bodies
Hurting and fighting each other
I don't want to think about it anymore.

-Full text of Divided Korea.1

This is a poem that shows miserable reality of divided Korea with metaphor. "There was no wrong,/ Fighting between themselves," means how absurd it is while mentioning self-examination. Honestly, it is deplorable that Korea was divided into two different countries by ideology. "Only bleeding/ without fighting against/ I don't want to hear it any more." It means that whatever caused the nation's division, we do not want to hear bleeding with no resistance. My understanding is that the poet tries hard to restrain her indignation. "Water flows from high to low,/ Runs to the river and sea" shows natural phenomenon. Who would dare go against the natural phenomenon. If there is anyone who tries to go against the natural phenomenon, they would meet a headwind. It is obvious that there is no dictator who can take it. Thus, it is true that a human cannot resist it. "The cold North West wind chilled Goes down and/ Takes the hand of the South Win/ There was no reason,/ Being divided into two bodies/ Hurting and fighting each other// I don't want to think about it any more." The cold North West wind means Jungil Kim, ruler of North Korea, and the South Wind means President of South Korea. Despite endeavors of Late President of South Korea, Daejung Kim, to meet Jungil Kim for peace, armed attacks and terrors of Jungil Kim to South Korea still continued. Thus, the poem suggests that North Korea is the most aggressive in the world. It makes sense considering the second Yunpyung naval battles in the west coast on June 29th, 2002, 2 years and 14 days later than inter-Korean summit on June 15th, 2000. Then, Steller's Sea Eagle (357 navy ship) of South Korea was attacked. What a tragedy! The poem suggests that a narrator in a poem has a clear and determined life philosophy.

Dancing bird 2.

　　—For flying highest—

　　To see farthest away
　　Have to fly the highest in the sky.

　　I have accepted, and endured patiently
　　Severe windstorms and air pressure
　　Evaporating misty air in clouds.

　　The world, I see from the highest sky
　　It is a small feather.
　　Round shapes, water drops.

　　It looks perilous, destroyed by footsteps,
　　And like the mighty blowing wind
　　Spreading many small sand castles

　　Inside there,

　　Ahong dahong* ahong dahong
　　Ahong dahong ahong dahong.

　　It is really funny.

* "Ahong dahong": a Korean mimetic word that describes human life, works or events in human relationships like marrying and divorcing, having fun, fighting and killing each other, laughing and crying over things in life. It means that human things look very significant in Korean.

We may understand the poem with common sense. However, it says that "To see farthest away/ Have to fly the highest in the sky." The dancing bird may mean a greedy person. It is obvious that we should fly high to see further and broadly. "Severe windstorms and air pressure/ Evaporating misty air in clouds." It is inevitable for a person to go through difficulties. "The world, I see from the highest sky/ It is a small feather./ Round shapes, water drops." As stated, the world or a person can show as a dot from the universe - i.e., a human is just an insignificant being. On the other hand, it is pathetic that people, the weakest existence in all the universe creation, show off and brag. "Inside there,/ Ahong dahong* ahong dahong/ Ahong dahong ahong dahong// It is really funny." It may mean that it is ridiculous for insincere people to feed off of their own prides and fool around with no care. This is a well-elaborated refined poem for them to self-exam themselves.

The song of earth

-Groaning sound of nature-

My body already raped
I want to die, my limbs are being torn apart.

Keeping a pure soul
Suffering from all kinds of pollutions
There persists one spot of hope like a thread.
As getting fall down
Try to get up
As getting become dirty
Try clean up more
Again, the stair of hopelessness,
One, two goes down
Making more move down,
However,
Cannot get up.
Cannot produce a life.
Cutting flesh in my deep heart

Ruining my metabolism and
Cannot making sing a warm, spring song
Cannot give birth to a life, one speck,
Rather, I want to die.
And leave my bleeding body here.

-Full text of The song of earth-

We call a celestial body where we live the earth. With one moon, the fourth planet of the solar system, the earth, rotates on its axis, while revolving around the sun through elliptical orbit. It was not until 16th century that we understood that the earth is round, rotates on its axis and revolves around the Sun.

Bo Kyung Kim, a poet, wrote a poem on the earth. She expresses her concern with the current and the future of the earth that has passed down through generations. On the other hand, considering that she looks at human beings from poetic perspective and mentions the earth hopelessly, she has special attention to the earth. Actually the special interest in and recognition of the current and the reality of the earth is the same as them to humans. It is a pathological phenomenon of the earth followed by environmental aggravation. However, humans do not destroy and damage the earth only. Heinous people's reckless and selfish behaviors result in the destruction and the damage. There is no reason for the earth to get damaged. Only humans do it. We should pay attention to it. Considering these, I would like to emphasize that the poem is very good from phenomenological and metaphysical perspectives.

"My body/ already raped" It depicts shameful tragic hurts from the beginning. "I want to die,/ my limbs are being torn apart." It becomes hopeless. "Keeping a pure soul/ Suffering from/ all kinds of pollutions/ There persists one spot of hope like a thread" Although the poetic narrator tried to possess clean and pure soul, there is no hope while suffered by various types of pollution and noise. The third and the fourth stanzas mention that the earth is dying with no hope to revive. It shows that the earth is reaching the last step not to be able to revive. Additionally, it is clearly stated that even deep down of the earth flesh is cut and the earth cannot carry a new life any more. "Rather,/ I want to

108

die./ And leave my bleeding body here./ To bleed from within the water vein of the earth." It depicts sincerely that the earth would like to die like a fable poem. It also describes that the earth bleeds from its water vein, which can be compared to flesh blood gushing out from blood vessel of a human. It is an extreme situation that there is no way to be soothed. For example, the poem describes the reality that heavily damaging the lands by recklessly digging up or plowing mountains or farmlands or cutting mountains for golf courses, ore development (mining) following mineral veins, residential land development, or road building. I understand that the poet's intention is to enlighten reckless vicious humans, while accusing greedy humans of destructive behaviors. It may be considered reckless violence of humans coming to the end.

On the other hand, it may be compared to humans. In particular, it may describe a woman in a hopeless situation. Thus, it may be very appropriate to compare the earth with the human body because tragic reality with tangible and intangible damages of the earth is very similar to that of humans. It is the truth of our society that cannot be concealed. Under these, I think that Bo Kyung Kim has great poetic ideas and excellent recognition of the reality.

This is an outstanding poem with excellent poetic embodiment, great poetic ideas, lively words and magnificently artistic senses. Therefore, it is one of the best poems that anyone would get empathized.

3. Conclusion

A poet is self-expression. From the perspective, it is necessary to examine how many of the world poets recognize the poem. For example, A. E. Houseman (1859-1936), a British poet, compares writing a poem with "a hurt pearl oyster making a pearl by secreting with a lot of pain. A biography of a writer including a poet shows that they write by embracing severe hardships that they go through and turning them into the great works.

The poetry world of "A Multicultural Song That I Sing Alone," a poem by Bo Kyung Kim, shows what we can learn from poems of other poets, but mostly unique trend of these poems. Thus, the distinctiveness of each of his poems enables us to think a lot.

Wordsworth defined a poet as "A poet is like a rock whose nature does not change. A poet is a supporter, a guardian and a warm-hearted person with love." in the preface of "Lyrical Ballads (1798)," one of his famous poetry that is the first poetry of romanticism. I agree with it considering that how difficult it is to write a poem and to become a poet.

You should keep in mind that a poem should use metaphors, pure images and the language of truth well. No metaphor cannot be a poem, because straight forward expression and realistic language like other proses including novels and essays cannot move readers. Thus, the metaphor is the life of the poem and emotion is the life of the poet because cold-hearted person cannot write anything whether it is a poem or a novel.

Therefore, it is important that the metaphor and the emotion are critical factors of a poem. From the perspective, there are a lot of great poems of the poet, Bo Kyung Kim. However, we investigated seven of his poems only under the space limit, although I regret not exploring more. Her fifth poetry book is well-balanced by lyricism with ontology. Thus, I think that it is very significant that her poetry covers nature and history. I wish the best for Bo Kyung Kim to succeed as a poet.

Gallery of Pictures

Author taught the dance, *Ganggangsuwollae*, to high school students, eight students representing Barrien County, in a county festival in Michigan in May, 2000.

Author taught the *Ganggangsuwollae* dance to
Korean American women in Michigan at Stony Creek
Park in August 1997, which they performed.

**Author taught the *Ganggangsuwollae* dance to
Korean American women in Michigan at Stony Creek
Park in August 1997, which they performed.**

High school students perform Ganggangsuwollae. Human, brothers, peace. Let's make one. Let's love together.

The author is dancing a solo peace dance for war victims.

Epilogue

In here, I spread the seeds of multicultural love, peace, dance, and song. From Asia to America to the whole word, from the origin of human history to today, from little things to great ones. Visible and invisible, looking for the gold vein of underground in languages, picking well ripened fruits, living as a fisherman of this land is very fun. Multiculturalism might be the ideal of human pursuits, as humans are not just single celled and have not just one sense of taste. Autumn time comes down slightly, seducing the green climax of summer and color of nature. The sky gets dark. Maybe the weather will change.

Bo Kyung Kim
Profile

Poet, Peace dancer, Former music teacher.

The author's original name is Soon Sil Kim. Author was born in Jeju in 1961, in South Korea, graduated from the Jeju National University's music department, became a music teacher, and taught music in a public junior high school in Jeju, Korea. After getting married and emigrating to the U.S., she taught all kinds of people from different racial backgrounds Korean traditional women's group dance, named Ganggangsuwollae. This dance was passed down from ancient societies, meant to prevent divorce and pursuing mult-racial harmony and unification, as the author taught in communities, schools, churches of Michigan, Ohio, and California.

And she also performed many solo dances to dedicate to war victims, using ancient Korean dances, sublimating it to peace dances, especially, one particular dance for the U.S. Civil War, which is performed in many places. She has also written many peace songs. In order to learn more about the U.S., she graduated from West Los Angeles College in liberal arts, and graduated with a second bachelor's in Political Science from Cal State Los Angeles. In 1995, she received the New Poet Prize from the Korean literature magazine "Munyesajo." She has published two books, and three Korean poetry books are in currently in the process of publication. Now, she is living in South Pasadena, California.

Bo Kyung Kim

Address
1711 Fremont Ave, South Pasadena, CA 91030.
email; bokim137@gmail.com, website; http://kimbokyung.net, Phone
number; 323-982-9356 (H), 323-551-7315(C)

CPSIA information can be obtained at www.ICGtesting.com
Printed in the USA
LVOW13*0014040214

372175LV00003B/132/P

9 781491 832202